Published in 2013 by The Rosen Publishing Group, Inc.
29 East 21st Street, New York, NY 10010

Photo Credits: **KEY** tc=top center; tr=top right; cl=center left; c=center; cr=center right; bl=bottom left; bc=bottom center; br=bottom right; bg=background
CBT = Corbis; iS = istockphoto.com; SH = Shutterstock; TF = Topfoto; wiki = Wikipedia
front cover iS; **4–5**cl SH; **6–7**c iS; **9**br, cr, tr TF; **10**bg SH; cr wiki; **11**c iS; **15**br SH; bc TF; **24**bc wiki; **24–25**c iS; **25**br, tr CBT; **26**bl SH; **26–27**cr SH; **28**tr iS; bc, br, tr SH; cl wiki; **29**br, cr, cr, tr iS; bc, c, c, tc SH

All illustrations copyright Weldon Owen Pty Ltd

Weldon Owen Pty Ltd
Managing Director: Kay Scarlett
Creative Director: Sue Burk
Publisher: Helen Bateman
Senior Vice President, International Sales: Stuart Laurence
Vice President Sales North America: Ellen Towell
Administration Manager, International Sales: Kristine Ravn

Library of Congress Cataloging-in-Publication Data

Coupe, Robert.
 The Great Wall of China / by Robert Coupe.
    p. cm. — (Discovery education: ancient civilizations)
 Includes index.
 ISBN 978-1-4777-0050-1 (library binding) — ISBN 978-1-4777-0085-3 (pbk.) —
 ISBN 978-1-4777-0086-0 (6-pack)
 1. Great Wall of China (China)—Juvenile literature. I. Title.
 DS793.G67C68 2013
 931—dc23

                                    2012019581

Manufactured in the United States of America

CPSIA Compliance Information: Batch #W13PK2: For Further Information contact Rosen Publishing, New York, New York at 1-800-237-9932

ANCIENT CIVILIZATIONS

THE GREAT WALL OF CHINA

ROBERT COUPE

PowerKiDS
press

New York

Contents

History of the Wall 6

Before the Wall............................8

The First Emperor........................10

The Qin Wall 12

Within the Wall 14

Mongol Invasion..........................16

The Ming Wall.............................18

Tools and Inventions.....................20

Defending the Wall.......................22

To the Present 24

Visiting the Wall 26

Fact File 28

Glossary.....................................30

Index 32

Websites 32

History of the Wall

The Great Wall of China is the longest structure ever built. It was constructed to protect China against attack from the north, and winds its way for about 4,000 miles (6,400 km) across the plains and mountains of northern China.

The first walls across parts of China were built as early as the fifth century BC. But it was not until the reign of the First Emperor, Qin Shi Huangdi, in the third century BC that the first "long wall" was built. Most of Qin's wall was made of rammed earth. By the fifteenth century AD, almost all of the old wall had fallen away. Under emperors of the Ming dynasty, a new wall—the one that is still standing today—was constructed.

Fifth century BC
China was divided into small states. The rulers of many of these states had walls of rammed soil constructed to protect their territory from attack.

The Qin dynasty
China became a unified country from 221 to 206 BC. Emperor Qin Shi Huangdi ordered a wall more than 3,100 miles (5,000 km) long built across northern China.

The Han dynasty
The wall was strengthened and extended. During this period (206 BC–AD 220), its total length reached 5,000 miles (8,000 km), the longest it has ever been.

The Sui dynasty
Much of the wall was rebuilt or repaired during the brief Sui dynasty (AD 581–618). But for 300 years afterward no further work was done on the wall.

The Ming wall

The wall built from 1445 to 1600, under the Ming dynasty, was an elevated roadway that connected forts. Parts of the Ming wall, which is not far from the Chinese capital, Beijing, have not been restored. In fact, much of it is in poor condition.

Map of the wall
The Great Wall was built bit by bit over many centuries and throughout the rule of many different dynasties.

Beijing

Yellow River

Xianyang

Yangzi River

EAST CHINA SEA

GREAT WALL
∿∿∿ Qin Dynasty
⎯⎯ Present Day

Minzhong•

e Jin dynasty
mies from Mongolia, to
e north, broke through
e wall during this period
15–1234). They invaded
ina and established the
an dynasty.

The Yuan dynasty
China and Mongolia were a single country. During the Yuan dynasty (1271–1368), no work was done on the wall. Much of it crumbled into ruins.

The Ming dynasty
The Mongols were driven out during this dynasty (1368–1644). A new and stronger wall of bricks and stone was built and kept in good condition.

Today
By the twentieth century, much of the wall had fallen into disrepair. Work from the 1950s onward has seen sections of wall repaired and opened to the public.

Before the Wall

The first dynasty, or line of rulers, in ancient China that we know about was the Shang dynasty. Its kings ruled parts of northern and central China until about 3,000 years ago. During this period, peasants grew crops and craftspeople used bronze, silk, jade, and other materials to make tools, weapons, clothing, and ornaments.

Eventually, warlike Zhou people from the northwest attacked and defeated the Shang. The Zhou dynasty lasted around 800 years, until the third century BC. It was a violent time, with many wars. Iron was used to make weapons, tools, and plows for agriculture. More and bigger cities were built, and merchants began carrying goods between them to trade.

Warring States period

During this period (475–221 BC), there were many clashes between armies. Powerful warlords forced many peasants to become soldiers. They rode into battle on horseback and used bows and arrows.

AGE OF BRONZE

During the Shang dynasty, artisans learned to work with bronze to make containers and ornaments. They poured the molten bronze into carved ceramic molds. When the bronze cooled, they broke the molds and polished the metal surface. Many of the bronze containers were decorated with complex designs.

Ancient finds
Archaeologists have discovered many statues, containers, jewelry, and other artifacts that date as far back as the Stone Age in ancient China.

Pottery jug
This red pottery jug, with two large handles and black spiral decorations, may be almost 3,000 years old.

Bronze bell
This highly decorated small bronze bell with pointed sides probably dates from the early years of the Shang dynasty.

Wine vessel
This bronze container for holding wine comes from the fourth century BC, during the later years of the Zhou dynasty.

Qin dynasty (221–206 BC)
Qin Shi Huangdi ruled China for only 11 years. He died in 210 BC. In 206 BC, a popular uprising overthrew his successor.

Did You Know?
The word China probably comes from *Qin*, which is pronounced "chin." The First Emperor's name lives on today, in the name of the country he unified.

Currency
Circular bronze coins with a square hole were used as money during this time. They were easy to carry on a string.

The First Emperor

At the end of the Warring States period (221 BC), the powerful king of the state of Qin, in northwest China, conquered the six other states. He, therefore, became the First Emperor of a unified China. He named himself Qin Shi Huangdi. *Shi* means "first," and *Huangdi* means "emperor and divine ruler."

Qin Shi Huangdi made many changes. He created strict laws, taxed everyone in the country, and introduced a single way of writing for all of China. He had roads and canals built. He ordered that walls that already existed in northern China be joined together to protect the newly united country against armies from Mongolia in the north. In this way, he created the first Great Wall of China.

Guarding the emperor
Thousands of life-size statues
of soldiers were placed in the
tomb of Qin Shi Huangdi to
guard and protect it.

Materials
Metal tools, such as knives and spades, existed, but most workers used simple timber tools or their bare hands to dig up rubble and soil, and carry stones and bricks.

Pounding soil
Workers probably used stones attached to wooden poles to pound soil and rubble together.

Carrying
Workers carried dirt and rubble from the nearby countryside to the section of wall that was being built.

Making bricks
Mud was put in wooden molds. They were left in the sun until the mud dried and hardened to form bricks.

The Qin Wall

Emperor Qin Shi Huangdi was a ruthless tyrant. He forced many of his subjects to work as slaves to build his wall. Peasants, prisoners, and soldiers were pressed into service. They worked ceaselessly through all seasons with little food and no protection from the weather. Many of them died from hunger, disease, or injury. In nine years, between 215 BC and 206 BC, these workers built 1,550 miles (2,500 km) of wall.

Much of the wall followed the line of earlier walls. Stones were used, especially in the mountainous regions, but most of the wall was made of soil and rubble rammed close together. Brick watchtowers were constructed at regular intervals along the wall. After the Qin dynasty collapsed in 206 BC, subsequent rulers of China extended and strengthened the wall.

Keeping watch
Archers kept watch from the towers along the wall. They used smoke, fire, and drumbeats to send messages.

At work on the wall

Workers formed human chains to pass building materials up the mountains or along the wall. They first built bamboo frames, which they filled with rammed soil as well as bricks, stones, and rubble.

Within the Wall

Before the Qin dynasty, when different parts of China were at war with each other, the people built huge walls around their land for protection. Armies of invaders from the north were also a constant threat. So were raiders on horseback, who swooped down on farms and stole or destroyed crops and animals. Some raiders carried off women and children. Others drove herds of grazing animals to rich pasturelands, then escaped north when they were pursued.

The Qin wall brought a new sense of security to the people of China, especially those in the north. It not only kept out intruders, it also allowed people to move more safely across the land. The wall made it possible for merchants to travel and to trade their goods.

That's Amazing!

The top of the wall was about 12 feet (3.7 m) wide. Four horses could be ridden side by side along it, and carts pulled along it. The wall came to be used as a type of highway.

Traders

Traders during the Han dynasty used camels to transport their goods westward from the ancient capital, Chang'an. The wall gave them shelter and protection.

TRADED GOODS

About 2,000 years ago, Chinese traders traveled long distances overland. They journeyed through northern India and eventually to Europe and Africa. Silk was their main product, but they also traded metals, tea, and spices. The routes they traveled are now known as the Silk Road.

Metal incense burner

Silk

Mongol Invasion

I n the early 1200s AD, Mongol armies led by Genghis Khan broke through the crumbling wall across northern China. By 1279, they had seized control of all of China, and it became part of a huge Mongol empire. Genghis Khan's grandson, Kublai Khan, had declared himself emperor in 1271 and became the first emperor of the Yuan dynasty.

The Mongol rulers spoke a different language from the Chinese. They dressed differently and had different social customs. They found it difficult to govern and control their Chinese subjects, who disliked and opposed them. A series of popular revolts forced them out of China after less than 100 years. But they and other groups continued their raids. So the leaders of the Ming dynasty, which replaced the Yuan dynasty, decided to build a new and stronger wall during the 1400s.

Mongol fighters

The mounted archers and lancers of the Mongol armies were highly disciplined. The Mongols captured vast areas, including all of China, other parts of Asia, present-day Russia, and northern India.

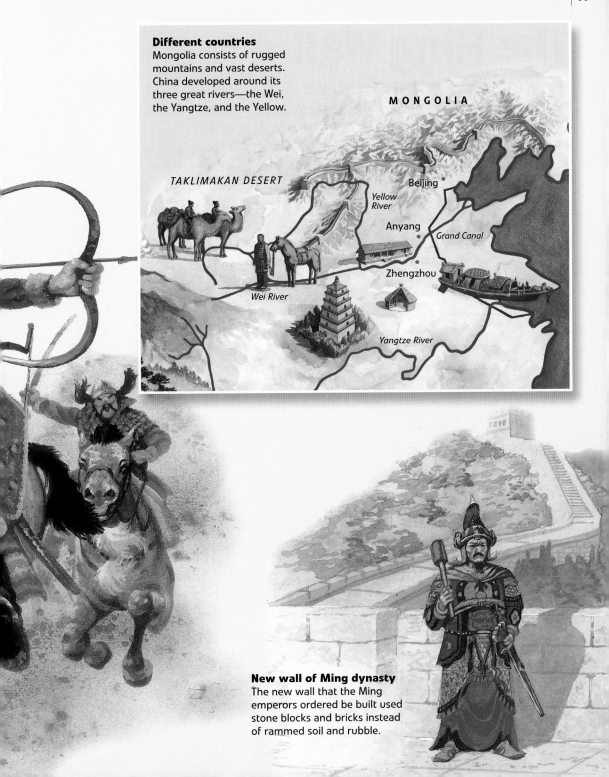

Different countries

Mongolia consists of rugged mountains and vast deserts. China developed around its three great rivers—the Wei, the Yangtze, and the Yellow.

MONGOLIA

TAKLIMAKAN DESERT

Beijing

Yellow River

Anyang

Grand Canal

Zhengzhou

Wei River

Yangtze River

New wall of Ming dynasty

The new wall that the Ming emperors ordered be built used stone blocks and bricks instead of rammed soil and rubble.

The Ming Wall

Zhu Yuanzhang came from a poor peasant family. In 1368, at the age of 40, he led a revolt against the Yuan dynasty and became the first emperor of the Ming dynasty. He is known as the Hongwu Emperor, and his dynasty ruled China until 1644.

Throughout the 1300s and the 1400s, war continued between the Chinese and the peoples to their north. In 1449, at the battle of Tumu, a Mongol army had a crushing victory over the Chinese and even captured the emperor. Soon after, the Chinese began building sections of a new wall. Work on this new wall went on during the fifteenth century and into the sixteenth century, until the sections were joined together to become the Great Wall that we know today.

Fact or Fiction?

Some people claim that it is possible to see the Great Wall of China from a spacecraft orbiting Earth. However, most astronauts say that this is impossible.

Stone and brick

Unlike the earlier wall of the Qin dynasty, the framework of the new wall was built mainly of stone and bricks. It was then filled in with a mixture of rocks, rubble, and soil, which was pounded until completely solid.

Building materials

Builders found materials as close as possible to the part of wall they were working on. Clay for bricks was usually nearby. But sometimes, blocks of stone had to be carried from distant quarries.

Stone

Large stone blocks were used at the base of the walls. They were cut from nearby quarries, then carried to the building site.

Bricks

The bricks were baked in extremely hot ovens called kilns. They were harder than the bricks dried by the heat of the Sun.

Bamboo

Bamboo grows in many parts of China. Workers tied bamboo poles together with rope to make ladders for scaling the walls.

Baskets

Thin strips of bamboo were used to weave baskets for transporting materials. Reeds and other plant materials were also used.

Tools and Inventions

Made in China

This illustration shows some of the everyday objects that appeared for the very first time in China. The Chinese also invented matches, gunpowder, and chess.

Many things that we use today were invented in ancient China. For example, the Chinese were the first to build a type of arched, stone bridge that let flood water through. They invented paper and a printing system. They had rudders to steer their boats about 1,000 years before Europeans started to use them. The first compass was Chinese. It consisted of a magnetic metal fish floating on water in a wooden container. The mechanical clock was also developed in China

Harness
The Han invented the harness, which went around a horse's chest, instead of its neck, to increase its pulling power.

Fishing reel
This came from a machine the Chinese used in battle to retrieve a javelin after it had been thrown at the enemy.

Wheelbarrows
These appeared in the first century AD, 1,300 years before Europeans had them.

Arched bridge
In AD 610, engineer Li Chun designed an arched bridge that was stronger and took less stone to build than other bridges.

Rudder
By the first century AD, Chinese boats had rudders for steering and controlling their direction.

The pulley
The Chinese realized that it takes much less energy to lift a heavy object if the lifting is done by a pulley.

One wheel
A pulley consists of a grooved wheel with a rope running inside the groove. The simplest system has only one wheel.

More wheels
A pulley with two or more wheels makes a weight even easier to lift. The more wheels, the heavier the weight that can be hoisted.

AT THE TOP OF THE WALL
The top of the wall was a type of highway. Horse-drawn carts carried goods, farm produce, and other materials from one tower to the next. Traders moved goods for long distances across the country. Soldiers and government officials marched or rode along it, too. Spouts on the northern side of the wall drained off rainfall.

Easy movement
Moving along the top of the wall was easier and safer than traveling across the countryside below, which was often rugged and steep.

Drains
Drains along the top of the wall collected rainwater and melted snow, which flowed out through spouts.

Wheelbarrow
Workers wheeled stones, bricks, and other materials up sloping surfaces and ramps to the top of the wall.

Besieging the wall
Enemies often used siege machines called trebuchets, which hurled boulders at the wall to smash it or to fall on the defending soldiers.

Smoke, fire, and the beat of drums were used to send messages to other towers along the wall.

Defending the Wall

While the Great Wall was maintained in good condition, it was an effective barrier against attack. Soldiers lived, worked, and kept watch in the towers along its length. Many of the towers were two stories high, with food and weapons stored inside. They contained stables for horses and rooms where the soldiers ate and slept.

There were sections along the wall where the towers were built just far enough apart that guards in one tower could fire arrows that reached halfway to the next tower. This meant that the guards could defend the wall even while they were inside the towers. During a full-scale attack, the soldiers took cover behind the battlements on the wall's northern side and rained down arrows on their attackers below.

Protection

Archers fought off attacks on the wall. They wore a helmet and thick armor that covered much of their body, but still let them move freely.

To the Present

In 1644, uprisings by the Manchu people to the northeast of China resulted in the Ming dynasty being replaced with the Qing dynasty, which lasted until 1911. Several decades of turmoil followed, until the Communist Party took control in 1949. For more than 300 years, almost no work was carried out on the wall. Much of it collapsed or crumbled in ruins.

In the 1950s, some restoration work was begun. However, in the late 1960s, there was another period of great strife, known as the Cultural Revolution. Violent gangs attacked long sections of the wall, blowing them up or knocking them down, and also removing stones to use for building materials. Today, attitudes have changed. Sections of the Great Wall are being repaired, and the Chinese regard it as an important symbol of their nation.

EARLY TWENTIETH CENTURY

This 1907 photograph shows a section of the wall winding through a rugged mountain region. Although the roadway is overgrown with long grasses and the road surface is eroded, this section appears to be in reasonable condition, with its battlements and towers still in place.

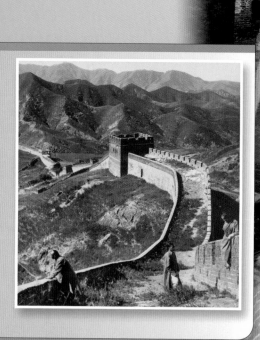

The Great Wall in 1907

Restored

This section of the wall, not far from Beijing, has been repaired in the last 30 years. Notice the two-story tower in the foreground and the gentle slope of the wide and shallow steps of the roadway.

Recent work

A great deal of work has been done since the 1980s to repair and rebuild broken parts of the wall. In some places, workers still use traditional methods and tools instead of modern machines.

Collecting soil and rubble
These workers, photographed in 1985, are gathering soil and rubble to rebuild a part of the wall at the eastern end.

Compacting
This man uses a heavy stone attached to a pole to pound soil and rubble until it is compacted into a solid mass.

Visiting the Wall

Tourists and other visitors have been able to visit sections of the wall since 1956, soon after restorations began. In 1972, US President Richard Nixon visited China and went to a part of the wall near Beijing. His visit was shown on television around the world. The publicity that resulted aroused great interest and encouraged people from many countries to travel to China to see the wall. In 1987, UNESCO declared the Great Wall a World Heritage Site. This means that it is considered a place of great historical and cultural importance to the world.

The number of people who visit the wall continues to increase every year. Most visitors go to one of the sections of the wall near Beijing. The nearest, and most popular, section is Badaling, about 50 miles (80 km) northwest of the city center. Once there, people can go up into the towers and walk along the roadway, from where they enjoy spectacular views of the surrounding countryside.

THE IMPERIAL PALACE

Another World Heritage Site in Beijing is the Imperial Palace, also known as the Forbidden City. This huge complex consists of many buildings containing a total of almost 1,000 rooms. It was home to the emperors of the Ming and Qing dynasties, and their courts, for almost 500 years. The Imperial Palace is surrounded by high walls and a deep moat.

One of the many halls inside the Imperial Palace

Badaling

Every year, millions of people visit the wall at Badaling. On weekends, crowds of people throng along the roadway there. But their numbers decrease once people start to climb the steeper parts of the wall.

Fact File

WONDERS

The Great Pyramid at Giza, in Egypt, was included in the Seven Wonders of the World, a list made by Greek travelers in the first and second centuries AD. The Qin Long Wall could not have been included in the list because the Greek travelers did not know it existed.

The Sphinx and Great Pyramid in Egypt

HADRIAN'S WALL

In AD 118, the Roman emperor Hadrian ordered a wall 73 miles (117 km) long be built across the width of what is now England. Hadrian's Wall aimed to keep tribes from the north out of the southern part of Britain, which was part of the Roman Empire.

A small fort on Hadrian's Wall

SATELLITE PICTURE

This picture of the Great Wall was taken from a satellite. It has been claimed that the wall can be seen from the Moon, but this is not true. From a spacecraft in orbit around Earth, it can probably not be seen by the naked eye.

A SURPRISE DISCOVERY

In 2009, a Chinese government mapping study revealed 180 miles (290 km) of the Ming wall that no one knew existed. Until then, this part of the wall had been hidden by hills or rivers, or it had been covered over by huge sandstorms that often swept over the region. Infrared range finders and GPS devices (like the one on the right) helped in this exciting new discovery.

MATERIALS

The wall was never built as a single construction. Both the Qin wall and the later Ming wall used parts of older walls and added to them. The Ming wall was mainly built of stone and brick. The Qin wall was made almost entirely of soil, leaves, hay, rubble, and mud. Workers pounded huge quantities of these materials together.

DANGEROUS WORK

Chinese people often refer to the Great Wall as "the longest cemetery on Earth." Especially at the time that the ancient Qin wall was being built, working conditions were extremely harsh, and some historians say as many as a million workers died. Many workers were convicted criminals who had been forced into service. Others were soldiers and peasants, who were also made to work on the wall.

DIMENSIONS

When it was built, the Great Wall was 16 to 25 feet (4.8 to 7.6 m) high. Now, some parts have worn away and are much lower. Originally, the wall ranged from 15 to 30 feet (4.6 to 9 m) wide at its base, and 9 to 12 feet (2.7 to 3.7 m) wide at the top. It varied depending on the type of terrain.

Glossary

archaeologist
(ahr-kee-AH-luh-jist) A person who investigates how people lived in the distant past by studying objects they left behind, for example, tools, weapons, jewelry, cooking pots, and items left in their tombs.

archers (AHR-cherz)
Soldiers who used bows and arrows as weapons.

armor (AR-mer)
Special clothing that soldiers wore in war to protect them from enemy weapons.

bamboo (bam-BOO) A long grass that has a hollow, woody stem. The ancient Chinese wrote on long strips of bamboo.

battlements (BA-tul-mentz)
Low walls at the top of towers or forts. Battlements had openings through which soldiers could fire their weapons.

bronze (BRONZ) A reddish metal that is made by mixing copper and tin, and sometimes lead.

canal (ka-NAL) A waterway created by humans that flows between natural waterways, such as seas or rivers.

civilization
(sih-vih-lih-ZAY-shun) A form of organized human society in which people live in cities or towns and share social customs and where there is some form of government. Arts and crafts and the existence of cities and agriculture are often signs of a civilization.

Cultural Revolution
(KUL-chuh-rul reh-vuh-LOO-shun) A period of strife and turmoil in China that lasted for about 10 years, until 1976. Many people were killed, imprisoned, or forced to move from their homes during this time.

dynasty (DY-nas-tee)
A period in which a country or region is ruled by members of the same family, who follow each other as rulers.

Genghis Khan
(JEN-gis KAHN) A Mongol leader and warrior who lived from about 1160 to 1227. He conquered most of Asia and parts of eastern Europe.

gunpowder (GUN-pow-dur) A mixture of chemicals in powder form that burn and explode when lit by a spark. Gunpowder is used in guns and fireworks, and for blasting rock.

incense (IN-sents) A kind of gum or other material that produces a perfume-like smell when it is burned. It is used in some religious ceremonies.

jade (JAYD) An extremely hard stone that can be green, white, red, or colorless. It is used for making jewelry, ornaments, and small statues.

kiln (KILN) A very hot oven or furnace that is used for baking mud to make bricks or clay to make pottery.

Kublai Khan
(KOO-bluh KAHN) The grandson of Genghis Khan, who conquered all of China and was Mongol emperor of China from 1271 to 1294.

Manchu people
(MAN-chew PEE-pul) People who came from the area to the northeast of China, east of Mongolia. This area, which was once called Manchuria, is now part of China.

merchant (MER-chunt)
A person who buys and sells or trades goods in order to make a profit. "Trader" is another word for "merchant."

molds (MOHLDZ)
Hollow containers into which liquid mud or clay is poured, then left to go hard. When the mud or clay hardens, it takes the shape of the mold.

Mongolia (mon-GOH-lee-uh)
A country in northern Asia between China and Russia.

peasants (PEH-zentz)
People who, in earlier times, grew crops and grazed animals on land they did not own. Peasants were usually very poor and had little education.

rudder (RUH-dur) A flat piece of wood attached to the back of a boat beneath the waterline. When it swings to one side or the other, it causes the boat to change direction.

satellite (SA-tih-lyt) An object that travels in orbit around a star or planet. The Moon is a satellite of Earth. Some satellites are spacecraft that take photos of Earth from space.

silk (SILK) A fine, soft cloth that is made from the cocoons of silkworms. The ancient Chinese were the first to make silk and Chinese merchants took it to other parts of the world.

Silk Road (SILK ROHD)
The name given to the routes over which merchants from China carried silk and other materials for trade overland as far as Europe and Africa.

Stone Age (STOHN AYJ)
The earliest period in which we know humans existed. Stone Age people used stone to make tools and weapons.

trebuchet (treh-byu-SHET)
A war machine, similar to a huge catapult, that was used to hurl large rocks and other heavy objects up into the air and over the walls of forts.

uprising (UP-ry-zing) A revolt by a large part of the population against the rulers of a country or a region.

warlord (WOR-lord)
A person who controls a part of a country and who commands an army that defends that area or tries to invade and take over other areas.

Index

A
archers 12, 16, 23
armor 23

B
Badaling, China 26, 27
bamboo 13, 19
battlements 22, 24
Beijing, China 7, 25, 26
bricks 7, 12, 13, 17, 18,
   19, 21, 29
bridge, arched 20
bronze 8, 9, 10

C
Chang'an 15
clock 20
coins 10
Communist Party 24
compass 20
Cultural Revolution 24

F
fishing reel 20

G
Genghis Khan 16
Great Pyramid 28

H
Hadrian's Wall 28
Han dynasty 6, 15

I
Imperial Palace 26
iron 8

K
Kublai Khan 16

L
Li Chun 20

M
Manchu people 24
merchants 8, 14, 15, 21
Ming dynasty 6, 7, 16, 17,
   18, 24, 26
Mongolia 7, 10, 17
Mongols 7, 16

N
Nixon, Richard 26

P
pottery 9
pulley 21

Q
Qin dynasty 6, 10, 12, 14, 18
Qing dynasty 24, 26

S
Shang dynasty 8, 9
Silk Road 15
Stone Age 9
Sui dynasty 6

T
trebuchets 22
Tumu, battle of 18

U
UNESCO 26

W
Warring States period 8, 10
wheelbarrow 20, 21

Y
Yuan dynasty 7, 16, 18

Z
Zhou dynasty 8, 9
Zhu Yuanzhang 18

Websites

Due to the changing nature of Internet links, PowerKids Press has developed an online list of websites related to the subject of this book. This site is updated regularly. Please use this link to access the list:
www.powerkidslinks.com/disc/gwall/